Alfred's Basic Piano Library

Prep Course

FOR THE YOUNG BEGINNER

Solo Book ◆ Level B

Willard A. Palmer ◆ Morton Manus ◆ Amanda Vick Lethco

Alfred Music
P.O. Box 10003
Van Nuys, CA 91410-0003
alfred.com

ISBN-10: 0-7390-0970-2
ISBN-13: 978-0-7390-0970-3

Illustrations by Christine Finn

Instructions for Use

1. This SOLO BOOK may be begun when the student has learned *GLIDING,* on page 8 of PREP COURSE LESSON BOOK B in ALFRED'S BASIC PIANO LIBRARY.

2. This book is coordinated page-by-page with LESSON BOOK B, and all assignments should be made according to the instructions in the upper right hand corner of the first page of each piece in the SOLO BOOK. It is not advisable, under any circumstances, to allow the student to move faster in the SOLO BOOK than in the LESSON BOOK, since the new principles that may be involved in each piece are best introduced in the pages of the LESSON BOOK.

3. The pieces in this book use ONLY the principles introduced in the corresponding LESSON BOOK. Only C POSITION and G POSITION are used. Melodic and harmonic intervals, from the 2nd through the 5th, are carefully reinforced. The student also begins to play pieces with HANDS TOGETHER. Slurs, ties, sharps and flats, as well as staccato playing, along with crescendos and diminuendos, all introduced in the Level B LESSON BOOK, are also reinforced.

4. Teachers who prefer a multi-key approach should not hesitate to have the student play any or all of these pieces in other five-finger positions, adding their own instructions about which notes are to be played flat or sharp. Students do not generally find this difficult, and the experience is invaluable.

5. Most of the pieces in this book have a DUET PART that may be played by the teacher, parent, or another student, on the same piano. The student frequently must play the solo part in a different octave, and this gives important experience at moving over the keyboard and playing in different keyboard areas.

6. When this book is combined with LESSON BOOK B and other corresponding materials available at this level, the teacher and parent may be assured that the student is receiving thorough training and more than adequate experience in all the principles covered in Level B.

THE PUBLISHER

Contents

4

Calendar Song

Use after GLIDING,
PREP COURSE Lesson Book B (page 8).

When you learn this song you will know
the number of days in each month!

Moderately

2nd time BOTH HANDS 1 octave LOWER

1. Thir - ty days has Sep - tem - ber, A - pril, June, and No - vem - ber.
2. Twen - ty eight; That's the ver - y short - est month, Feb - ru - ar - y,

All the rest have thir - ty one; Feb - ru - ar - y stands a - lone.
And you add just one day more When the year di - vides by four.

DUET PART

1st time 8va; 2nd time as written

Play a Little Samba!

Use after BALLOONS (page 9).

Brightly

1. Sam - ba, sam - ba; Play "A Lit - tle Sam - ba!"
2. Sam - ba, sam - ba; You will love the sam - ba.

Here's a song you'll real - ly like to play.
You will love to play it ev - 'ry day!

DUET PART (Student plays 2 octaves higher.)

BOTH HANDS 8va

6

Use after COME AND PLAY! (page 11).

Puppies and Guppies

Moderately fast

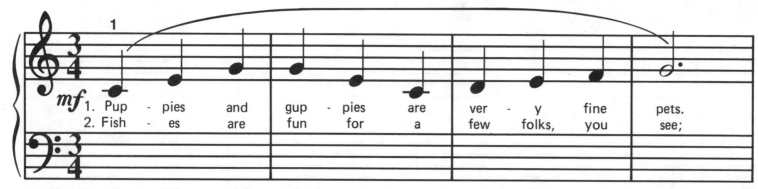

mf

1. Pup - pies and gup - pies are ver - y fine pets.
2. Fish - es are fun - pies for a few folks, you see;

mf

Pup - pies are play - ful, and gup - pies are wet.
Oo - dles of poo - dles and are bet - ter for me!

5

DUET PART (Student plays 1 octave higher.)

RH

LH *mp*

sempre staccato

Our Team

Use after WHAT CAN WE DO? (page 13).

Brightly

2nd time BOTH HANDS 1 octave higher

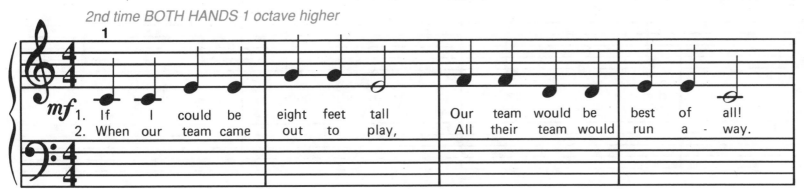

1. If I could be eight feet tall Our team would be best of all!
2. When our team came out to play, All their team would run a - way.

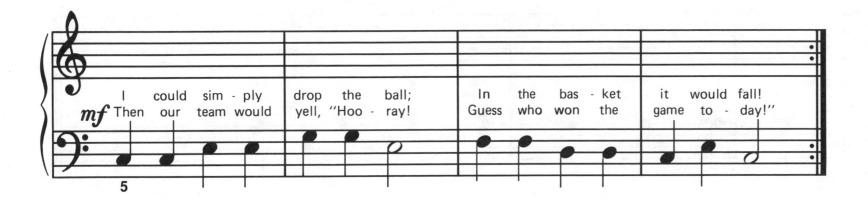

I could sim - ply drop the ball; In the bas - ket it would fall!
Then our team would yell, "Hoo - ray! Guess who won the game to - day!"

DUET PART (Student plays 1 octave higher 1st time; 2 octaves higher 2nd time.)

2nd time 8va

Chopsticks, Anyone?

Use after TAKING TURNS (page 16).

Moderately fast

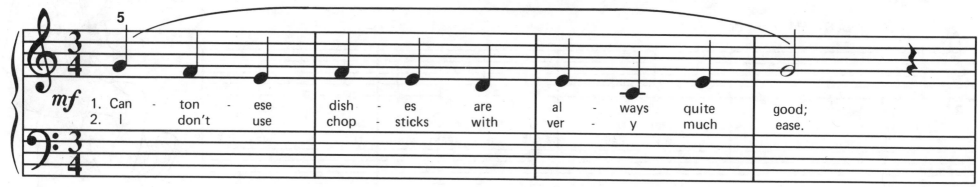

1. Can - ton - ese dish - es are al - ways quite good;
2. I don't use chop - sticks with ver - y much ease.

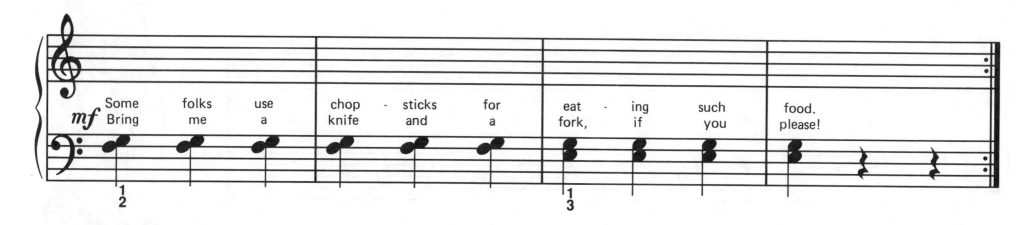

Some folks use chop - sticks for eat - ing such food.
Bring me a knife and a fork, if you please!

DUET PART (Student plays 2 octaves higher.)

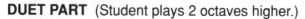

If I Won Ten Million Dollars

Use after ROCKETS (page 18).

Use after LET'S HAVE FUN! (page 21).

Penguins on Parade

Merrily

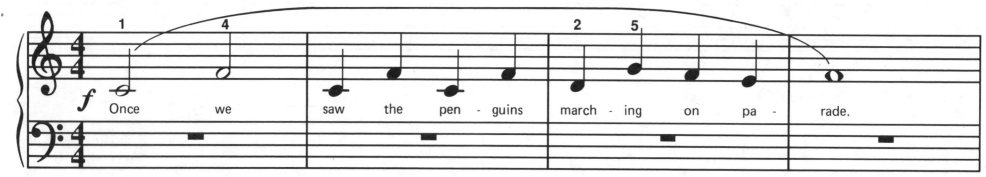

Once we saw the pen - guins march - ing on pa - rade.

DUET PART (Student plays 1 octave higher.)

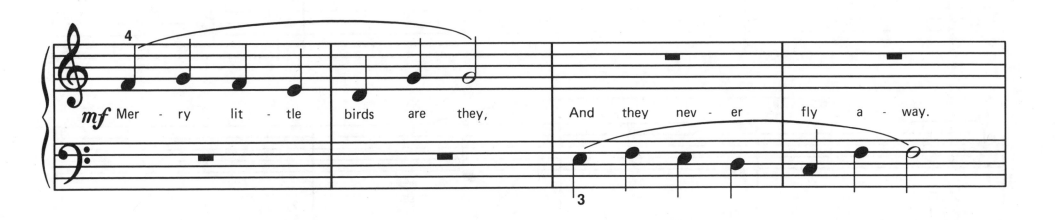

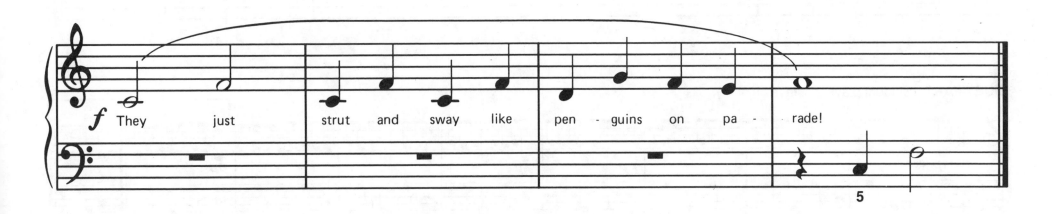

Use after GROWING UP! (page 25).

Music Makes Me Glad!

Happily

1. Mu - sic al - ways makes me glad!
2. Just play mu - sic when you're blue.

Mu - sic nev - er makes me sad.
It will make you hap - py too!

DUET PART (Student plays 2 octaves higher).

Use after AIRPLANES (page 28).

Buy a Balloon!

Moderately fast

1. Buy a bal - loon!
2. Buy a bal - loon!

p Buy a bal - loon!
Buy a bal - loon!

Or - ange and and red, small and ones, yel - low and and blue.
Big ones and and shin - y and and new!

DUET PART (Student plays 2 octaves higher.)

Use after LITTLE THINGS (page 29).

My Big Bass Drum

Moderately fast

2nd time BOTH HANDS 1 octave LOWER

1. If I could play in the march - ing band, I'd
2. And ev - 'ry time we'd go march - ing by, You'd

play on my big bass drum. (Bum - bum!)
hear me play, "rum - tum - tum." (Bum - bum!)

DUET PART (Student plays 1 octave lower 1st time; 2 octaves lower 2nd time.)

Clowns!

G POSITION

Use after "MOON-WALK" (page 31).

Bright and bouncy

1. Crowds of clowns are com - ing, 'cause the cir - cus is in town.
2. Strut - ting, stum - bling, trip - ping, tum - bling, flip - ping, fall - ing down;

Big ones, small ones, Romp - ing all a - round,
Short ones, tall ones, Ev - 'ry kind of clown!

DUET PART (Student plays 1 octave LOWER.)

Play DUET PART 1 octave HIGHER

THANKS to Dmitri Kabalevsky!

Tons of Fun!

G POSITION

Use after JINGLE BELLS! (pages 32-33).

Not too slow

Play BOTH HANDS 1 OCTAVE LOWER

1. What do the el - e - phants do for fun,
2. May - be they frol - ic and jump for and run,
3. Each of them hav - ing a ton of fun!

When there is no - bod - y with 'em?
Danc - ing in el - e - phant rhy - thm!
Would - n't you love to be with 'em?

*Repeat once,
then play page 17*

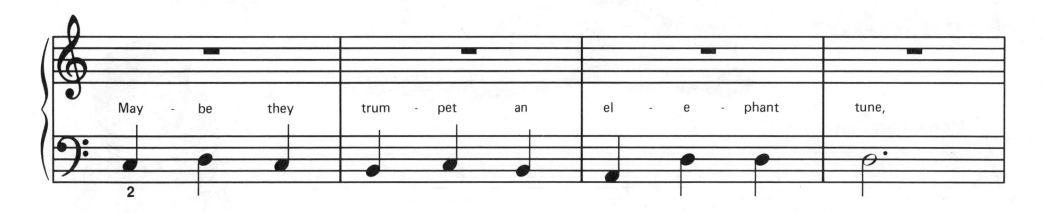

May - be they trum - pet an el - e - phant tune,

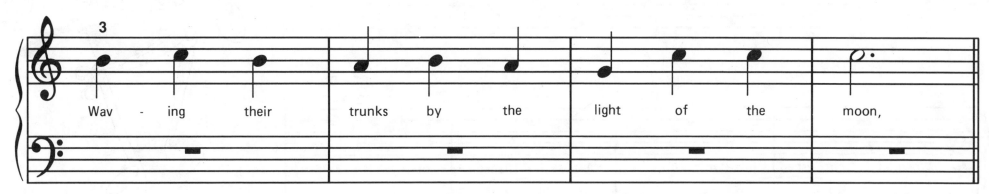

Wav - ing their trunks by the light of the moon,

PLAY THE 1st PAGE AGAIN!

DUET PART

mf *fine*

D.C. al fine

18

My Robot

Use after MAKE TIME FOR MUSIC! (page 35).

Moderately fast

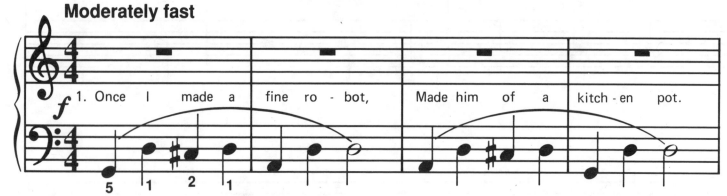

1. Once I made a fine ro-bot, Made him of a kitch-en pot.

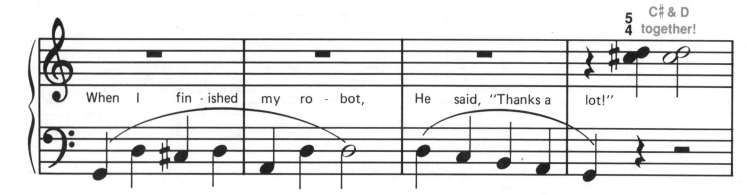

When I fin-ished my ro-bot, He said, "Thanks a lot!"

$\frac{5}{4}$ C# & D together!

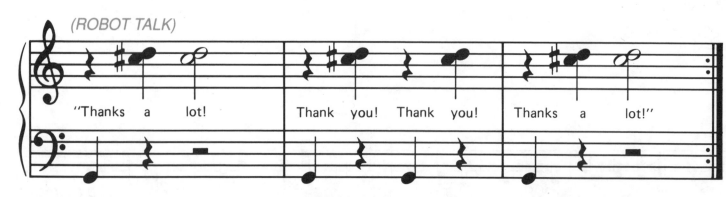

(ROBOT TALK)

"Thanks a lot! Thank you! Thank you! Thanks a lot!"

2nd Verse:
"Hope you don't think I am rude,
But please bring me something good.
Pots are programmed to hold food.
Bring me all you've got!"
"Thanks a lot!" *etc.*

3rd Verse:
If you make a new robot,
Please don't use a kitchen pot.
He'll eat all the food you've got,
And say, "Thanks a lot!"
"Thanks a lot!" *etc.*

3rd time gradually dying away - - - - - - - - -

Television

C POSITION REVIEW

Use after ROCKIN' TUNE (page 36)
or MARCHING SONG (page 37).

Moderately slow

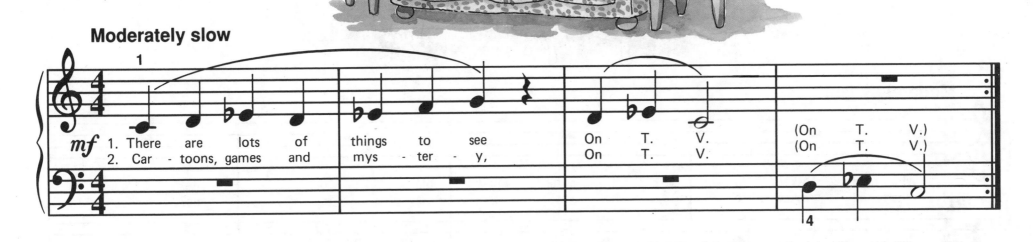

mf
1. There are lots of things to see On T. V. (On T. V.)
2. Car - toons, games and mys - ter - y, On T. V. (On T. V.)

f When you're watch - ing, do not slouch; No, no, no! (No, no, no!)

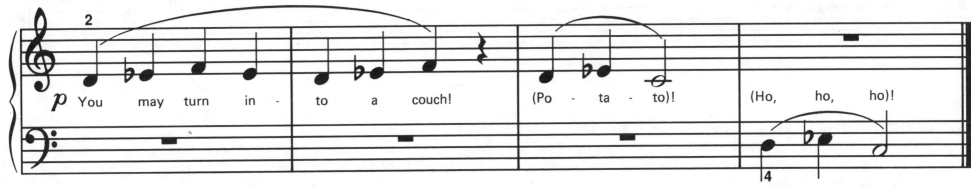

p You may turn in - to a couch! (Po - ta - to)! (Ho, ho, ho)!

One octave lower - - -

Sí, Sí, Sí!

Use after INDIAN SONG (page 38)
or MUMBO-JUMBO (page 39).

Moderately fast

mf

When I asked "Jo - sé, if he would play for me,
When I asked "Jo - sé, what will would you play play for for me, me?"

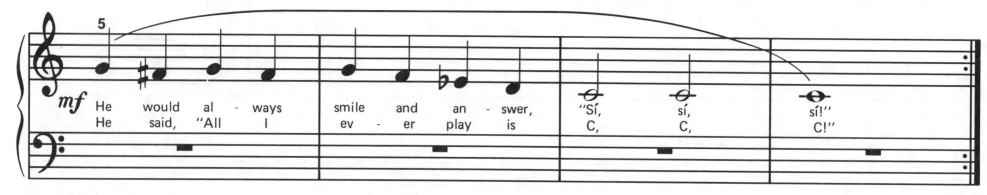

mf

He would al - ways smile and an - swer, "Sí, sí, sí!"
He said, "All I ev - er play is C, C, C!"

FOR DUET: This piece may be played as a ROUND. The student plays 1 octave higher.
The 2nd part is played 1 octave lower than written, beginning when the student reaches the 3rd measure.
Both parts make the indicated repeat. The player of the 2nd part will have two measures (C, C, C) to play
after the student finishes.

Use after CRACKER JACK! (page 41).

Popcorn Popping!

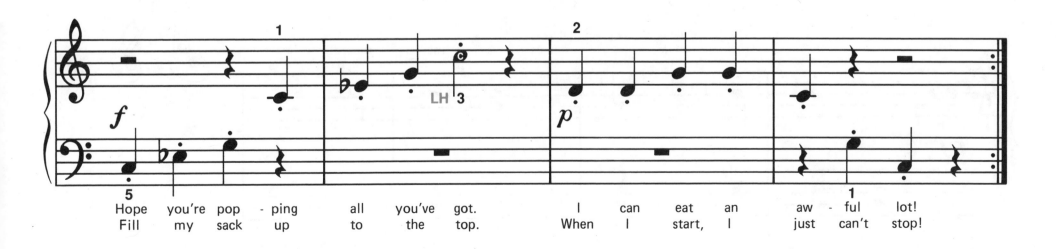

Happily

Cross LH over RH!

1. Pop - corn pop - ping, pip - ing hot!
2. How I love to hear it pop!

Pop - ping in the pop - corn pot.
When it's pop - ping, see it hop!

Hope you're pop - ping all you've got.
Fill my sack up to the top.

I can eat an aw - ful lot!
When I start, I just can't stop!

22

Use after ANYONE FOR TIC-TAC-TOE? (page 43).

I'm a Puppet!

G POSITION REVIEW

Brightly

1. If you pull on these lit - tle strings,
2. You can pull an - y string you please;

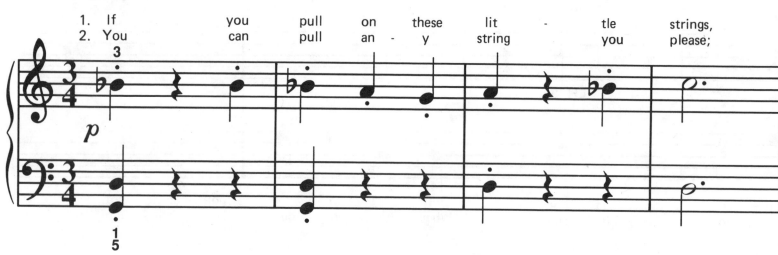

I will do man - y clev - er things.
(All but this one. It makes me sneeze.)

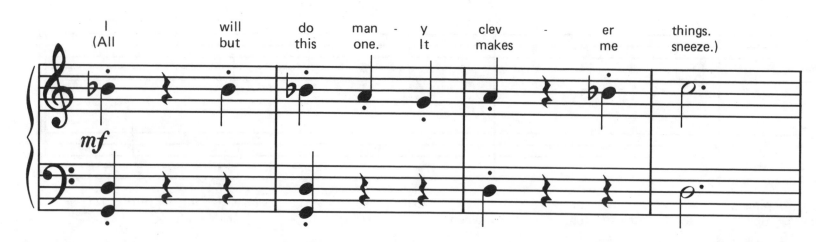

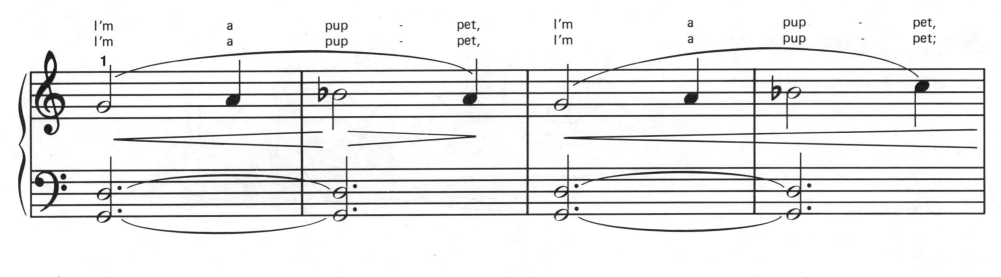

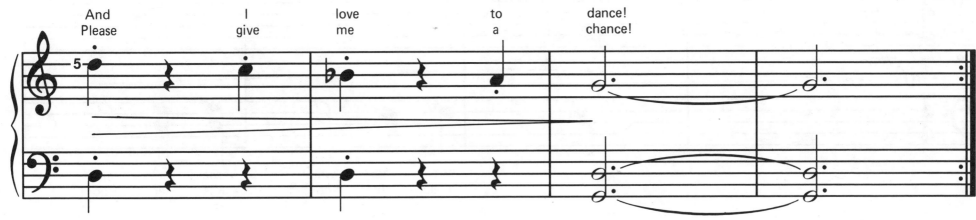

DUET PART (Student plays 1 octave LOWER.)

2nd time play DUET PART 8ᵛᵃ

THANKS to Charles Gounod!

24

See You Later!

C POSITION & G POSITION REVIEW*

Use after CELEBRATION (pages 44-45).

Cheerfully

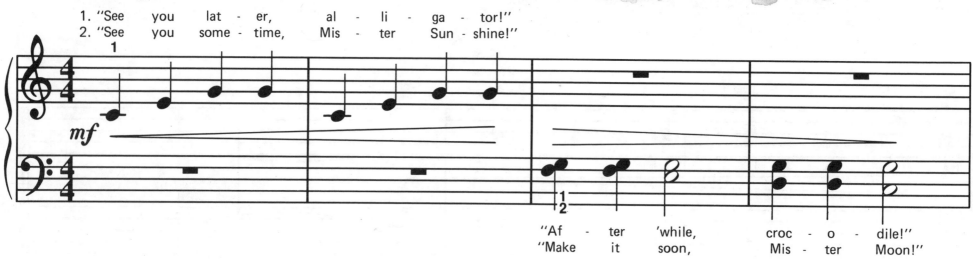

1. "See you lat - er, al - li - ga - tor!"
2. "See you some - time, Mis - ter Sun - shine!"

"Af - ter 'while, croc - o - dile!"
"Make it soon, Mis - ter Moon!"

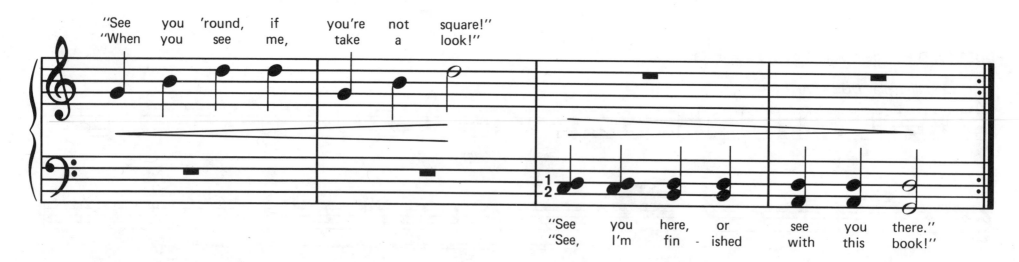

"See you 'round, if you're not square!"
"When you see me, take a look!"

"See you here, or see you there."
"See, I'm fin - ished with this book!"

*Can you tell which line is in C POSITION, and which line is in G POSITION?